STUDY PLANNER

D -

MOOD ☺ ☺ ☺ ☹ ☹	DATE.	MON	TUE	WED	THU	FRI	SAT	SUN

TODAY'S PRIORITY

○

○

○

PLAN		TOTAL TIME	H	M
	○	6		
	○	7		
	○	8		
	○	9		
	○	10		
	○	11		
	○	12		
	○	1		
	○	2		
	○	3		
	○	4		
	○	5		
	○	6		
	○	7		
	○	8		
	○	9		
	○	10		
	○	11		
		12		
		1		
		2		
		3		
		4		
		5		

COMMENT

STUDY PLANNER

MOOD 😊😊😐😟😣	DATE.		MON	TUE	WED	THU	FRI	SAT	SUN

TODAY'S PRIORITY

- ○
- ○
- ○

PLAN			TOTAL TIME	H	M
	○	6			
	○	7			
	○	8			
	○	9			
	○	10			
	○	11			
	○	12			
	○	1			
	○	2			
	○	3			
	○	4			
	○	5			
	○	6			
	○	7			
	○	8			
	○	9			
	○	10			
	○	11			
		12			
COMMENT		1			
		2			
		3			
		4			
		5			

STUDY PLANNER

D -

MOOD ☺ 😐 ☹ 😦 😫	DATE.	MON	TUE	WED	THU	FRI	SAT	SUN

TODAY'S PRIORITY

○

○

○

PLAN		
		○
		○
		○
		○
		○
		○
		○
		○
		○
		○
		○
		○
		○
		○
		○
		○
		○
		○
		○
		○
		○

TOTAL TIME	H	M
6		
7		
8		
9		
10		
11		
12		
1		
2		
3		
4		
5		
6		
7		
8		
9		
10		
11		
12		
1		
2		
3		
4		
5		

COMMENT

STUDY PLANNER

MOOD ☺☺☺☹☹	DATE.	MON	TUE	WED	THU	FRI	SAT	SUN

TODAY'S PRIORITY

○

○

○

PLAN		
		○
		○
		○
		○
		○
		○
		○
		○
		○
		○
		○
		○
		○
		○
		○
		○
		○
		○
		○

TOTAL TIME	H	M
6		
7		
8		
9		
10		
11		
12		
1		
2		
3		
4		
5		
6		
7		
8		
9		
10		
11		
12		
1		
2		
3		
4		
5		

COMMENT

STUDY PLANNER

D -

MOOD ☺ ☺ ☺ ☹ ☹	DATE.		MON	TUE	WED	THU	FRI	SAT	SUN

TODAY'S PRIORITY

○

○

○

PLAN			TOTAL TIME	H	M
		○			
		○	6		
		○	7		
		○	8		
		○	9		
		○	10		
		○	11		
		○	12		
		○	1		
		○	2		
		○	3		
		○	4		
		○	5		
		○	6		
		○	7		
		○	8		
		○	9		
		○	10		
		○	11		
			12		
			1		

COMMENT

	2		
	3		
	4		
	5		

STUDY PLANNER

D -

MOOD 😊 😄 😐 🙁 😣	DATE.	MON	TUE	WED	THU	FRI	SAT	SUN

TODAY'S PRIORITY

○

○

○

PLAN				TOTAL TIME	H	M
	.	○		6		
		○		7		
		○		8		
		○		9		
		○		10		
		○		11		
		○		12		
		○		1		
		○		2		
		○		3		
		○		4		
		○		5		
		○		6		
		○		7		
		○		8		
		○		9		
		○		10		
		○		11		
				12		
				1		
				2		
				3		
				4		
				5		

COMMENT

STUDY PLANNER

D -

MOOD ☺😄😐🙁😫	DATE.	MON	TUE	WED	THU	FRI	SAT	SUN

TODAY'S PRIORITY

○

○

○

PLAN			TOTAL TIME	H	M
		○			
		○	6		
		○	7		
		○	8		
		○	9		
		○	10		
		○	11		
		○	12		
		○	1		
		○	2		
		○	3		
		○	4		
		○	5		
		○	6		
		○	7		
		○	8		
		○	9		
		○	10		
		○	11		
			12		
COMMENT			1		
			2		
			3		
			4		
			5		

STUDY PLANNER

D -

MOOD ☺☻☺☹☹	DATE.		MON	TUE	WED	THU	FRI	SAT	SUN

TODAY'S PRIORITY

○

○

○

PLAN		○
		○
		○
		○
		○
		○
		○
		○
		○
		○
		○
		○
		○
		○
		○
		○
		○
		○
		○
		○
		○

TOTAL TIME	H	M
6		
7		
8		
9		
10		
11		
12		
1		
2		
3		
4		
5		
6		
7		
8		
9		
10		
11		
12		
1		
2		
3		
4		
5		

COMMENT

STUDY PLANNER

MOOD ☺ ☺ ☺ ☹ ☹	DATE.	MON	TUE	WED	THU	FRI	SAT	SUN

TODAY'S PRIORITY

○

○

○

PLAN	
	○
	○
	○
	○
	○
	○
	○
	○
	○
	○
	○
	○
	○
	○
	○
	○
	○
	○
	○
	○

TOTAL TIME	H	M
6		
7		
8		
9		
10		
11		
12		
1		
2		
3		
4		
5		
6		
7		
8		
9		
10		
11		
12		
1		
2		
3		
4		
5		

COMMENT

STUDY PLANNER

D -

MOOD ☺☺☺☹☹	DATE.		MON	TUE	WED	THU	FRI	SAT	SUN

TODAY'S PRIORITY

○

○

○

PLAN		
		○
		○
		○
		○
		○
		○
		○
		○
		○
		○
		○
		○
		○
		○
		○
		○
		○
		○
		○
		○

TOTAL TIME	H		M	
6				
7				
8				
9				
10				
11				
12				
1				
2				
3				
4				
5				
6				
7				
8				
9				
10				
11				
12				
1				
2				
3				
4				
5				

COMMENT

STUDY PLANNER

D -

MOOD ☺ ☻ ☺ ☹ ☹	DATE.		MON	TUE	WED	THU	FRI	SAT	SUN

TODAY'S PRIORITY

○

○

○

PLAN		TOTAL TIME	H	M
	○	6		
	○	7		
	○	8		
	○	9		
	○	10		
	○	11		
	○	12		
	○	1		
	○	2		
	○	3		
	○	4		
	○	5		
	○	6		
	○	7		
	○	8		
	○	9		
	○	10		
	○	11		
		12		
		1		
		2		
		3		
		4		
		5		

COMMENT

STUDY PLANNER

D -

MOOD ☺☺☺☹☹	DATE.	MON	TUE	WED	THU	FRI	SAT	SUN

TODAY'S PRIORITY

○

○

○

PLAN		
		○
		○
		○
		○
		○
		○
		○
		○
		○
		○
		○
		○
		○
		○
		○
		○
		○
		○
		○
		○

TOTAL TIME	H	M
6		
7		
8		
9		
10		
11		
12		
1		
2		
3		
4		
5		
6		
7		
8		
9		
10		
11		
12		
1		
2		
3		
4		
5		

COMMENT

STUDY PLANNER

D -

MOOD ☺☺☺☹☹	DATE.	MON	TUE	WED	THU	FRI	SAT	SUN

TODAY'S PRIORITY

○

○

○

PLAN			TOTAL TIME	H	M
		○	6		
		○	7		
		○	8		
		○	9		
		○	10		
		○	11		
		○	12		
		○	1		
		○	2		
		○	3		
		○	4		
		○	5		
		○	6		
		○	7		
		○	8		
		○	9		
		○	10		
		○	11		
			12		
COMMENT			1		
			2		
			3		
			4		
			5		

STUDY PLANNER

D -

MOOD ☺☺☺☹☹	DATE.	MON	TUE	WED	THU	FRI	SAT	SUN

TODAY'S PRIORITY

- ○
- ○
- ○

PLAN		○
		○
		○
		○
		○
		○
		○
		○
		○
		○
		○
		○
		○
		○
		○
		○
		○
		○
		○

TOTAL TIME	H	M
6		
7		
8		
9		
10		
11		
12		
1		
2		
3		
4		
5		
6		
7		
8		
9		
10		
11		
12		
1		
2		
3		
4		
5		

COMMENT

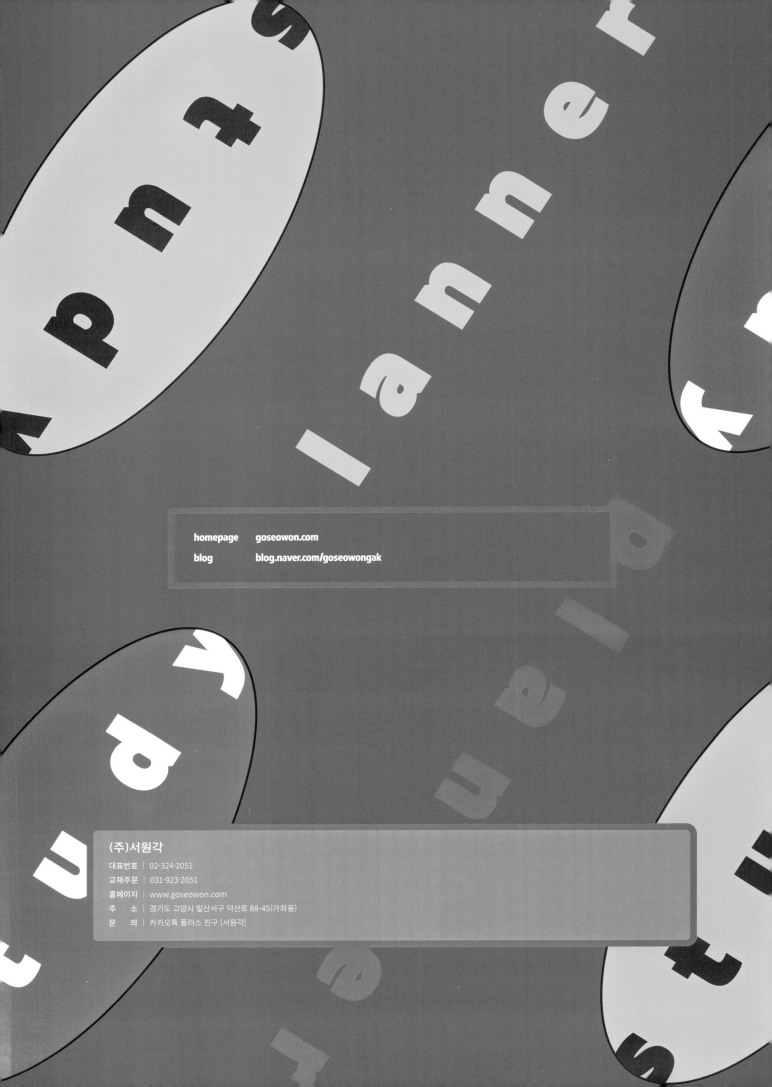

homepage   goseowon.com
blog   blog.naver.com/goseowongak

(주)서원각

대표번호 | 02-324-2051
교재주문 | 031-923-2051
홈페이지 | www.goseowon.com
주   소 | 경기도 고양시 일산서구 덕산로 88-45(가좌동)
문   의 | 카카오톡 플러스 친구 [서원각]